SHARK
WHALE
OCTOPUS
MORAY
JELLYFISH
DOLPHIN
ORCA
STARFISH
SEA SLUG

Millions of years ago, everything that lived on Earth lived in the ocean. This was where all life began, and to this day there are more creatures there than anywhere else in the world. Beneath the waves there exists a kaleidoscope of life-forms, many of which have remained unchanged for millions of years.
Many sea creatures are almost too small to see, while others have become undersea giants. Some even look like they should be alien life-forms! Prepare to be impressed, prepare to be scared—above all, prepare to be amazed!

PREDATORS
BELOW THE WAVES

Most creatures under the waves are predators, eating some other (usually smaller) creatures in order to survive. Of all the predators in the world's oceans, sharks are perhaps the most feared. Having evolved more than 400 million years ago, sharks ranging in size from 6in to 65ft long (15cm to 15m) now inhabit our oceans.

While most undersea predators' preferred weapon may be teeth, many use powerful venom for defense and sometimes attack: stingrays and lionfish, for example.

Weighing up to 5,000lbs (2,250kg) and reaching over 20ft (6m) in length, great white sharks are the largest known predatory fish on the planet.

GREAT WHITE SHARK

LEMON SHARK

Lemon sharks have very poor eyesight but they compensate with an excellent sense of smell and electrical field detectors.

Sharks will often bite just out of curiosity!

FROM THE SHALLOWS TO THE DEEP

GIANT GROUPER

Size: 6–9ft (2–2.7m)
Where: Indian and Pacific Oceans
Features: Solitary, slow swimmers
which eat shellfish and fish.

BARRACUDA

Size: 4–7ft (1.2–2m)
Where: Tropical Atlantic and Pacific
Features: Very fast and agile, large tail.

SHARK
RAY
BARRACUDA
GROUPER
MORAY

MORAY EEL

Size: 3–11ft (1–3.5m)
Where: Reefs and rocks
Features: Long, muscular
body. Few or no fins apart
from dorsal fin. Tubular
nostrils to detect prey.

STINGRAY

Stingrays hide just under the sandy ocean floor,
waiting to strike. Be careful where you walk–they
have a venomous sting in their tail.

SHARKS There are more than 400 species of sharks alive today, but fewer than 10 species are dangerous to humans.

UNDERSEA FACTS Some sharks need to keep moving nearly all the time because swimming helps them to breathe.

UNDERSEA GIANTS

Undersea giants living today include the largest creature known to man: the blue whale. At up to 110ft (33.5m) long and 181 tons in weight it is believed to be the largest animal ever to have existed. Even though these whales may be the biggest of creatures, they live entirely on the smallest: plankton (microscopic sea organisms) and tiny shrimps called krill.

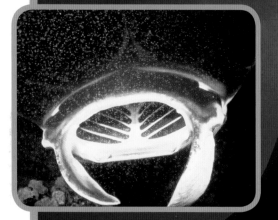

HUMPBACK WHALE

The humpback whale (main picture) has a distinctive body shape with long pectoral fins and a knobbly head. It is an acrobatic animal, often breaching the surface to slap back down in dramatic style.

MANTA RAY

Size: up to 25ft (7.5m) across
Where: Tropical waters
Features: Pair of "horns" used to guide krill into its mouth.

FROM THE SHALLOWS TO THE DEEP

HUMPBACK
GIANT SQUID
WHALE SHARK
MANTA RAY

The giant squid is a deep ocean dweller similar to the octopus pictured here. A creature of myth and legend, giant squid can grow to some 43ft (13m) in length.

WHALE SHARK

The whale shark is a filter feeding shark and is the largest living fish species. This distinctively marked shark is found in tropical and warm oceans around the world.

WHALES use underwater sound waves called sonar to communicate to other whales across many miles of ocean.

UNDERSEA FACTS Whales are mammals that give birth to live babies. A blue whale calf measures 23ft (7m).

open these pages to enter your . . .

UNDERSEA 3-D

PANO

RAMA

The Atlantic spotted dolphin is found in the Gulf Stream of the North Atlantic Ocean.

Some species of sea creature are very social, living in family groups, and hunting and playing together. The highly developed behavior, of dolphins and orcas for example, makes training and bonding with these wonderful creatures a really rewarding experience.

TOP PERFORMERS

Older Atlantic spotted dolphins have a very distinctive spotted coloration all over their body.

DOLPHIN ORCA SEA LION

The orca or killer whale is the largest species of the oceanic dolphin family. It is found in all the world's oceans, from the cold Arctic and Antarctic regions to warm, tropical seas. Orca are versatile predators feeding on fish and marine mammals, including sea lions, seals, and even large whales.

SEA LION

Sea lions have long front flippers, and can walk on four flippers on land. Their range extends from the subarctic to tropical waters of both the Northern and Southern hemispheres.

Some species of sea lions are readily trainable and are often a popular attraction at zoos and aquariums. Sea lions have been trained by the US Navy's Marine Mammal Program, based in San Diego.

FROM THE SHALLOWS TO THE DEEP

DOLPHINS can jump as high as 16ft (5m) out of the water.
They land on their back or sides.

UNDERSEA FACTS An average bottlenose dolphin lives for about 25 years, although some have been known to reach the age of 40.

Coral reefs are marine structures produced by living organisms in warm, shallow seas. In most reefs, the main organisms are stony corals that make an exoskeleton (shell) of calcium carbonate. The Great Barrier Reef, which runs for 1,250 miles (2,000km) beside Australia's east coast, is probably the best known. But these fragile ecosystems are under attack, with human activity causing the greatest problem. In particular, pollution and over-fishing pose the most serious threat. Destruction of reefs by boats and shipping traffic is also a major problem.

REEF LIFE

BUTTERFLY FISH

There are approximately 115 species of butterfly fish found mostly on the reefs of the Indian, Atlantic, and Pacific Oceans.

CANDY-CANE STARFISH

Starfish are able to regenerate lost arms. A whole new starfish may be regenerated from a single arm attached to a portion of its central body.

PUFFERFISH

Pufferfish are the second most poisonous vertebrate in the world, the first being a golden poison frog. The skin and certain internal organs are highly toxic to humans, but nevertheless the meat of some species is considered a delicacy in both Japan (as fugu) and Korea (as bok-uh).

SEA HORSE

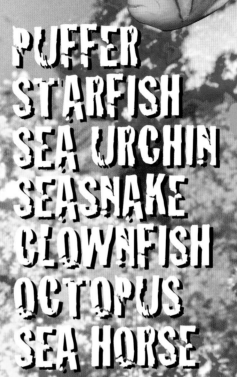

CLOWNFISH

PUFFER
STARFISH
SEA URCHIN
SEASNAKE
CLOWNFISH
OCTOPUS
SEA HORSE

ANEMONE FISH

SEA URCHIN

Sea urchins are small, globular, spiny sea creatures. They are found in oceans all over the world.

OCTOPUS

Venomous sea snakes are found from the Indian Ocean to the Pacific. All must come to the surface regularly to breathe.

FROM THE SHALLOWS TO THE DEEP

BANDED SEA SNAKE

GROUPERS can weigh up to 900lbs (400kg) and grow to 9ft (2.7m) in length.

UNDERSEA FACTS Giant groupers are a fairly common sight in shallow tropical waters. They feed on lots of marine life including small sharks.

UNDERWATER ALIENS

SEA ANEMONE

There are more species of life under the waves than above. The sheer variety of weird and wonderful creatures is incredible, and because much of the deepest ocean has yet to be explored, who knows what waits to be discovered? All shapes, sizes, and colors exist in this incredible undersea world.

RED SEA URCHIN

Sea slugs are carnivorous, eating sea sponges and other soft-bodied marine life—including other sea slugs!

SEA SLUG

BASKET STAR

Basket stars like this one are in fact a type of starfish. Many of them have arms with many branches. They generally live in deep seas and can have arms measuring 28in (70cm) and grow to 6in (15cm) across.

LEAFY SEA DRAGON

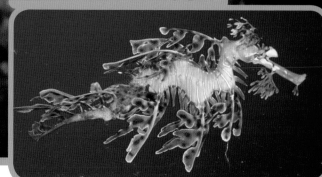